Modern hockey started
in the middle of the 1800s.

T0082134

field

/feeld/

In field hockey you have hockey sticks and a ball.

You hit the ball with the hockey stick.

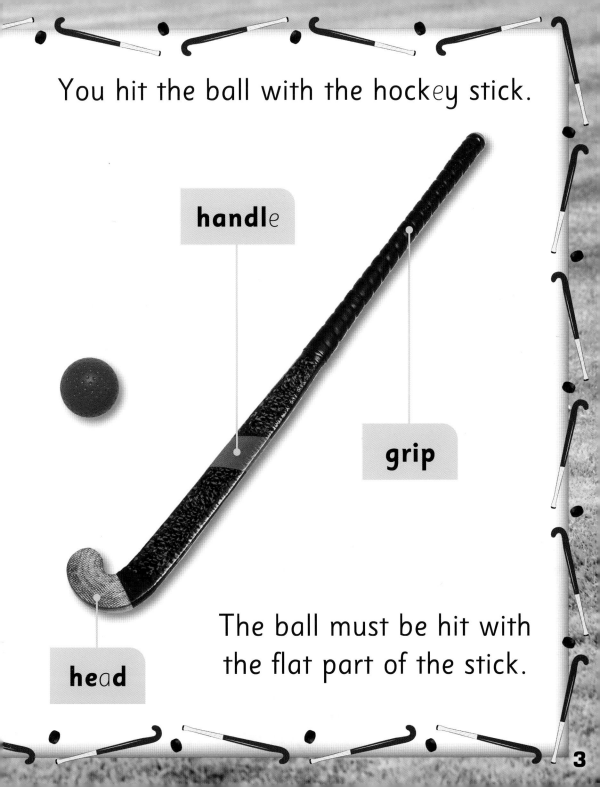

handle

grip

head

The ball must be hit with
the flat part of the stick.

team players
/teem **plai**erz/

goalkeeper

There are ten players and
a goalkeeper on a team.

Attackers attempt to score goals and defenders attempt to stop the opposite team scoring goals.

A hockey ball is solid
plastic and very hard!

You must have
shin and mouth guards.

You need guards and padding as it is very painful to be hit with a hockey ball!

The goalkeeper must stop
the ball entering the goal net.

They need lots of padding too.

If you are a goalkeeper, you can stop the ball with your body as well as the stick.

ice
/ies/

This is an ice hockey rink.

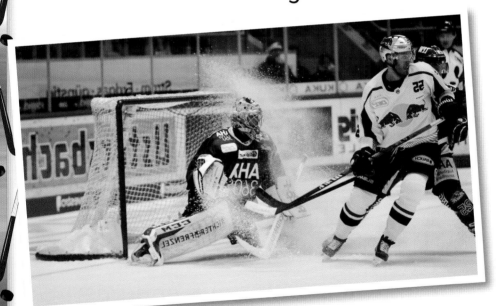

Ice hockey is very quick.

The sticks are much longer and
you have to have helmets, guards,
and plenty of padding.

For ice hockey, you need
a rubber puck, not a ball.

Pucks are stored in the freezer
before matches, as they then
stick better to the ice.